INDIAN RHINOS
AND THEIR BABIES

MARIANNE JOHNSTON

The Rosen Publishing Group's
PowerKids Press™
New York

Special thanks to Diane Shapiro of the Bronx Zoo for making this project possible.

Published in 1999 by The Rosen Publishing Group, Inc.
29 East 21st Street, New York, NY 10010

First Edition

Book Design: Resa Listort

Photo Credits: All photos © Wildlife Conservation Society.

Johnston, Marianne.
    Indian rhinos and their babies/ by Marianne Johnston.
            p.   cm. — (A zoo life book)
    Includes index.
    Summary: Describes the characteristics of the Indian rhinoceros and how mother Indian rhinos living in zoos are taught to care for their babies.
    ISBN 0-8239-5318-1
    1. Indian rhinoceros—Juvenile literature. 2. Indian rhinoceros—Infancy—Juvenile literature. 3. Zoo animals—Juvenile literature.
[1. Indian rhinoceros. 2. Rhinoceros. 3. Animals—Infancy. 4. Zoo animals.] I. Title. II. Series: Johnston, Marianne. Zoo life book.
    QL737.U63C735 1998
    599.66'8—dc21   98-7668
                                                                                                          CIP
                                                                                                          AC

Manufactured in the United States of America

CONTENTS

THE RHINOCEROS

There are five **species** (SPEE-sheez), or kinds, of rhinoceroses. One species, the Indian rhino, lives in the countries of Nepal and India. Most rhinos live in Africa and Asia. Many rhinos that once lived in the wild now live in protected parks in their homelands.

So many Indian rhinos have been killed that they are now **endangered** (en-DAYN-jerd). Zoos around the world are trying to save Indian rhinos by raising them in **captivity** (kap-TIH-vih-tee).

ORDER:
PERISSODACTYLA
FAMILY:
RHINOCEROTIDAE
GENUS & SPECIES:
RHINOCEROS UNICORNIS

◀ Indian rhinos feed on grass, fruit, leaves, and twigs.

WHAT ARE INDIAN RHINOS LIKE?

Indian rhinos have thick, folded skin that makes them look like they are wearing armor. Fully grown male Indian rhinos can weigh up to 6,000 pounds. Most Indian rhinos have a large horn that sticks out of the top of their snout. Some wild rhinos are **dehorned** (dee-HORND) to keep them safe from **poachers** (POH-cherz). Poachers kill rhinos for their **valuable** (VAL-yoo-bul) horns.

Indian rhinos live in forests, where they can munch on grass and plants. They also eat twigs and leaves from shrubs and small trees. Indian rhinos love to **wallow** (WAH-loh) in water. Splashing and rolling around in muddy water helps rhinos cool off.

Not only does mud keep a rhino cool, but it also protects its skin from insects. ▶

RHINOS AT THE ZOO

Most people have never seen an Indian rhino. In fact, there are only about 50 of these rare animals in zoos around the world.

Zookeepers do their best to give rhinos a lot of space to live and move around. A rhino's zoo **habitat** (HA-bih-tat) is made to look as much like its natural habitat as possible. Trees and a muddy watering hole are two things that make an Indian rhino habitat perfect.

When zoos give Indian rhinos a good place to live, the rhinos are more likely to stay healthy and **breed** (BREED).

Indian rhinos are good swimmers. In the wild they can swim easily across wide rivers.

GIVING BIRTH IN THE WILD

Rhinos give birth to one baby at a time. A female Indian rhino is **pregnant** (PREG-nunt) for sixteen months. That's almost a year and a half!

When an Indian rhino gives birth in the wild, she finds a very private place. A spot in a forest surrounded by small trees is a perfect setting for an Indian rhino to have a baby.

Tall grass near swampy areas also gives the mother privacy. Once she finds the right spot, the mother rhino gives birth by herself.

A female Indian rhino is pregnant for almost ▶ twice as long as a human female.

A RHINO BIRTH
AT THE ZOO

When zookeepers find out one of their Indian rhinos is pregnant, there is much excitement. The world needs more Indian rhinos since they have become an endangered species.

During the pregnancy, zookeepers make sure the female Indian rhino is healthy and eating well. A few weeks before she gives birth, zookeepers separate her from any other rhinos. The mother is also taken away from the main **exhibit** (eg-ZIH-bit) area so that she won't be bothered by visitors to the zoo. Rhinos in the wild are alone most of the time. When a mother Indian rhino gives birth, she doesn't want any other animals near her.

Indian rhinos are shy and prefer to be by themselves. This is especially true for a female rhino who is ready to give birth.

THE BIRTHING AREA

In most zoos, animals have an indoor habitat as well as their exhibit area outside. This is true for Indian rhinos as well. The indoor habitat is used when a female Indian rhino is close to giving birth. Zookeepers want her to give birth in a place where she is comfortable. When a rhino is about to give birth, nobody wants her to be nervous or scared.

Zookeepers don't want to bother a mother-to-be unless she needs help. Some zoos set up a small camera by the indoor area. A television connected to the camera lets zookeepers outside watch the pregnant rhino to make sure she is okay. This way the mother Indian rhino has the privacy she needs.

A young Indian rhino stays close to its mother for the first two to three years. ▶

HERE COMES THE BABY

Finally it is time for the birth. The mother walks around her birthing pen. She grunts as she tries to push her **calf** (KAF), or baby, out of her body. When the calf is just about to come out, the mother Indian rhino lies down on her side.

The baby struggles out. Then the baby takes its first breath. Just after her baby is born, a mother Indian rhino stands up and begins licking the calf clean.

After about an hour, the baby can stand and **nurse** (NERS), or drink its mother's milk.

◀ This baby rhino was born in a zoo. The baby's mother and grandmother were also born at the zoo.

THE FIRST FEW MONTHS

For the first few days of its life, a baby rhino follows its mother very closely. In the wild, **predators** (PREH-duh-terz), such as tigers, often try to catch and eat young rhinos.

Even though rhinos in zoos don't have to worry about tigers, Indian rhino calves still stay close to their mothers. A baby rhino remains in a private area for about a month after it is born. When it is strong enough, it can be taken to the exhibit area, where zoo visitors can see it.

18

Did you know that a newborn rhino can weigh almost 150 pounds? ▶

GROWING UP AT THE ZOO

Baby rhinos grow very fast. By the time they are one year old, they weigh 1,500 pounds! For the first year or two of its life, a baby rhino drinks its mother's milk. By the time an Indian rhino calf is six months old, it will be eating some regular food too, such as grass and leaves.

Rhino calves stay close to their mothers for about two or three years. At two or three years old, rhino calves are able to take care of themselves.

As it gets older, a rhino calf might try carrots and apples.

THE FUTURE OF THE INDIAN RHINO

It is against the law to kill Indian rhinos. Sadly, poachers still break these laws and kill Indian rhinos for their horns. Some people pay lots of money for the horns. They believe medicines made with them have special powers.

Today only about 2,000 Indian rhinos are left in the world. You can help them by visiting and supporting zoos all over the world. Zoos help bring baby Indian rhinos into the world. These little rhinos are the future of their species and will help keep the Indian rhino from becoming **extinct** (ek-STINKT).

WEB SITE

You can learn more about Indian rhinos at this Web site: http://www.rhinos-irf.org/rhinos/indian.html

GLOSSARY

breed (BREED) To have babies.

calf (KAF) A baby Indian rhino.

captivity (kap-TIH-vih-tee) When an animal lives in a zoo instead of the wild.

dehorned (dee-HORND) An animal whose horn has been removed.

endangered (en-DAYN-jerd) When something is in danger of no longer existing.

exhibit (eg-ZIH-bit) An area of a zoo where a certain animal can be seen by visitors.

extinct (ek-STINKT) When a certain kind of animal no longer exists.

habitat (HA-bih-tat) The surroundings where an animal lives.

nurse (NERS) When a baby drinks milk from its mother's body.

poacher (POH-cher) A person who illegally kills animals that are protected by the law.

predator (PREH-duh-ter) An animal that kills other animals for food.

pregnant (PREG-nunt) When a female animal has a baby or babies growing inside her body.

species (SPEE-sheez) A group of animals that are very much alike.

valuable (VAL-yoo-bul) Important, or worth lots of money.

wallow (WAH-loh) To roll around in mud or muddy water.

INDEX